This page belongs to

_____

Copyright © 2025, Deborah Means

Published by Johnson Tribe Publishing, LLC, Atlanta, GA

All rights reserved, including the express right to reproduce this book or portions thereof in any form whatsoever, whether now known or hereinafter developed. This book may not be copied or reproduced without the express written permission of the authors or publisher. The author is also available for speaking engagements and may be contacted at debbie.means16@gmail.com .

Manufactured in the United States of America

ISBN: 979-8-9925000-3-5

FIRST EDITION -

USA $ $15.99

# DEDICATION

I dedicate this book to my mom, Vivian Means, who recognized some journalistic tendencies in me as a kid and has always encouraged me to be a writer.

# ACKNOWLEDGEMENTS

I want to acknowledge the many children's book authors, such as Beverly Cleary, Barbara Park, Eric Carle, and others, who inspired me to become an author. I would also like to thank the teachers who taught me and the students I've had the pleasure of training and imparting to. Many of those experiences have shaped the ideas that I write about.

I'd also like to thank all those who contributed to the creation of this book.

Darla is 7 years-old and in the second grade.

Darla LOVED spending time with her family.

Darla LOVED playing with her pets.

Darla loved lots of things,
but there WAS something that she didn't like.

Darla
HATED VEGETABLES!!!!
ALL KINDS OF VEGETABLES!!!!

Every day during dinner, Darla would get rid of the vegetables on her plate.

ON MONDAY,
she gave Pumpkin,
the cat, her green peas.

ON TUESDAY,
she gave Muffin, the dog, her carrots.

ON FRIDAY,
when her Mom wasn't looking, she fed the broccoli
to her baby brother.

# Later that Night,

As she slept in bed, she had a dream.
Each vegetable visited her in the dream.

"Why did you give us to the cat? We keep your heart happy and pumping strong".

Darla jumped out of bed and ran to look for Pumpkin, the cat. She was standing on the window sill. Her heart was happy and pumping strong.

She ran down to the basement to see Muffin, the dog. Muffin was running around playing with her ball. She could see in the dark!

She went to the cat's playroom and found Skeeter enjoying his catnip without sneezing.

She went to her sister's room and found Hermie, the hamster in his cage combing his shiny, silky fur and taking selfies.

She went to the kitchen and found the baby not sitting in his highchair but holding it over his head. He winked at her and smiled.

Darla was AMAZED!!!

She couldn't wait until dinner time.

"Oh boy, Im really going to eat my vegetables now!"

### FINALLY, ON FRIDAY,
Darla's Mom prepared broccoli for dinner.  Not only did Darla get broccoli, but so did the baby.  They both ate ALL of the broccoli on their plates.

Before she went to bed, Darla looked in the mirror. She felt terrific! She looked fabulous!

"Vegetables are the bomb!!"

She grabbed her phone, smiled, and took a selfie. Then Darla went to bed.

As Darla slept that night, the vegetables came back in a dream. This time, they were cheerful and merry. They were having a vegetable parade!!

Darla's baby brother was leading the pack in the front as the drum major. The green peas were playing drums. The carrots were blowing trumpets. The corn was holding colorful balloons. The lima beans were waving flags that said, "Vegetables are the bomb!". The broccoli was doing flips and splits.

## ABOUT THE AUTHOR

Deborah Means is a native Atlantan. She has served as an early childhood educator in Atlanta, Cobb County, and Douglas County, Georgia, for many years. She comes from a family of educators. Her precious childhood and teaching experiences have served as the mirror for most of her writing ideas.

Deborah graduated from Benjamin E. Mays High School in Atlanta, GA, and then obtained a Bachelor's degree from Tuskegee University in Tuskegee, AL. Deborah received a Master's degree from Mercer University in Atlanta, GA. She has completed programs of study at Georgia State University and has received many certifications and awards in her field.

Deborah is an Alpha Kappa Alpha Sorority, Inc. member and enjoys meeting the community's needs in various capacities.

Deborah is a member of World Changers Church International. As a believer in Jesus Christ, she has been anointed by God to be a light for others in the kingdom of God.

www.ingramcontent.com/pod-product-compliance
Lightning Source LLC
Chambersburg PA
CBHW061401090426
42743CB00002B/107